The Trib

A Panegyrical F

Philo

Alpha Editions

This edition published in 2024

ISBN : 9789362097132

Design and Setting By
Alpha Editions
www.alphaedis.com
Email - info@alphaedis.com

As per information held with us this book is in Public Domain.
This book is a reproduction of an important historical work. Alpha Editions uses the best technology to reproduce historical work in the same manner it was first published to preserve its original nature. Any marks or number seen are left intentionally to preserve its true form.

Contents

DEDICATION, TO THE HONORABLE THE LADY ANN COKE. ....- 1 -
TO THE READER. ....- 3 -
THE TRIBUTE. ....- 4 -
FOOTNOTES ....- 17 -

DEDICATION,
TO THE HONORABLE
THE LADY ANN COKE.

PRAISE—when it is fairly earned and justly due, is that meed which virtue delights to bestow upon merit; and, as it is highly gratifying to every worthy mind to receive, so next to those who merit it, it is to none more delightful than to those who are allied to, and love and regard the object of the Eulogy. Most grateful then must it be to the feelings of a beloved wife, to hear and even read of the honorable and praise-worthy actions of a kind and tender husband. It is indeed like the oil of gladness to the heart, which, while it softens and lubricates, rejoices and refines: while it is read it delights—inspires a desire to imitate—infuses a portion of the spirit it celebrates into the bosom of rectitude—and cherishes the noble incentive to "go and do likewise." Under this impression it is, that the Author has presumed to dedicate to your Ladyship, this humble tribute of his respect and esteem. If he must not be allowed to rank it with the brighter effusions of imagination; yet, being founded in truth, it is intrinsically superior to the flights of fancy, and he trusts when you consider the justness of the panegyric, and the sincerity which inspires it; you will look over the imperfection of the Performance, in regard to the goodness of the intention; and readily pardon the writers defects of genius in justice to the warmth of his feelings.

Should this humble attempt tend to circulate more widely the Virtues it aspires to praise, or induce some more elevated Bard to

> "Touch the sounding strings,
> And in more fervid pœans sing his fame."

the Author will be highly gratified and rejoice in the happy effects of his labours.

He begs most respectfully
to subscribe himself,
your Ladyship's very obedient,
humble Servant,
PHILO.

TO THE READER.

The principal part of the following little Poem (if it deserves so high a character) was composed ten or a dozen years ago, and is extracted from a much longer Eulogy upon our Great Patriot, his Holkham, and his Agriculture; but which, for reasons not necessary to mention here, has never met the public eye; nor would what is here published, have done so now, had the Author been aware of any Competitor in the same field, who had attempted to do justice to the great and good man whose fame he aspires to sing. But now the Guardian of our County's rights, her liberties and laws, has resigned his seat in Parliament, and after seeing the great measures for which he so long contended in the House of Commons (namely, a Reform in the Representation—a repeal of p. viii the Corporation and Test Acts—and the destruction of the rotten Boroughs;) granted to the energetic exertions of a great People, aided by the support of a Patriotic Monarch, and a wise Ministry; has retired to the Sylvan shades of his wide domain, to enjoy the well earned meed of public virtue and private spirit; the Author could no longer delay presenting this humble tribute to his fame, and he trusts it will now be deemed neither misplaced nor ill timed, and although its pretensions are so humble, yet as they are ardent and sincere, he hopes it will be received with the candour and indulgence such trifles (while they survive) are usually received, when the praise is so justly due—so dearly earned—and so seldom deserved; in which case he will be highly gratified and his labour amply rewarded.

PHILO.

North Walsham, Dec. 25th, 1832

THE TRIBUTE.

YES—BRITONS BOAST! in these dark times to know
A man whose Virtue gilds the world below;
And, like the glory of the Northern star,
Is known, admired and gazed at from afar;
Who though he shines so high above his kind,
Is Polar light to Peasantry and Hind;
And yet his county, to her lasting shame,
No Bard has roused to eulogize his name;
To paint the Virtues in a mortal shrine,
And point the gem by its refulgent shine.
So be it mine to touch the sounding string,
The FRIEND; the PATRIOT; and the MAN to sing.
O could I reach the famed Apollo's lyre;
I'd chaunt his praises with a Poets fire;
But if unequal to such lofty flights,
My subject warms me, and my task delights;
And though unused to raise the tuneful song,
The MIGHTY THEME shall make my numbers strong;
Bright TRUTH shall guide me, like the solar rays,
Illume my darkness and direct my praise!
Inspire each thought, and breathe in ev'ry line,
And grace my Eulogy with rays divine;
And, while I paint the scene, the fact recite,
Still burst upon me in a blaze of light.

Wake then my MUSE the gen'rous trump of fame,
And let her clarion laud the Patriot's name;
Whose glorious actions well deserve the lay,
In deathless strains his merits to pourtray;
Who, while he makes his much loved HOLKHAM smile,
Exalts the glory of our Sea girt Isle.
What though short lived, my tribute I will bring,
And add my feather to the Eagle's wing;
Upon his pinions striving, thus to climb,
Upborne awhile along the stream of time,

And tho' my garland may fall off, his plumes
A grateful Muse her transient song presumes.

See the great FARMER at his rural seat,
When cares of state admit of his retreat;
Within his noble hospitable dome,
The Prince as well as Peasant finds a home;
Born for the *world* and for his race designed,
His Godlike bounty flows for all mankind;
Receives the Stranger, as a welcome guest,
Who while he tarries, feels no wish unbless'd;
The Patriot there with gay and cheerful heart,
Mid' all his greatness has the happy art,
To set each timid visitor at ease,
By courteous manners ever apt to please;
Where, open as his hand, th'expanding door,
Receives the wealthy where he feeds the poor;
Where none are seen to sorrow or complain;
Within the circle of his wide domain,
Abundance reigns; and comfort sweetly flows;
And, like the shadow, follows where he goes:
No discontent is felt when he is nigh,
And anxious cares before his presence fly;
The faithful hind rejoicing in his smile,
With cheerful industry pursues his toil;
The gen'rous rustic glories in his sight,
Who makes his heavy burden weigh more light;
And feels exalted and rejoiced to find;
The best of masters of the human kind;
Proud of his kindred, then he seems to scan,
His inbred worth, and deems himself a man.

O if the man who makes a single blade,
Lift its green head above the parched glade;
Where never verdure did before appear,
Deserves the plaudits of the world to hear;
What shall we say of him whose arts contrive,
To make whole fields of smiling herbage thrive;

Who turns the moor, into a fertile vale,
Where flocks and herds inhale the vernal gale;
Congeals the sand upon the northern breeze
And decorates the waste with shrubs and trees:
Such worth as this should like the sunbeams blaze,
And sculptur'd marbles speak to sing his praise;
Fame raise him pillars in each land and clime,
And Poets praise him in the song sublime;
The deathless laurel round his temples twine,
And his immortal wreath untarnish'd shine.

* * * * *

On lib'ral terms his Tenants are posses'd,
Their contracts made, they feel themselves at rest;
Their tenures permanent, at easy rents,
None make a bargain which he e'er repents;
But once engaged, he finds his contract please;
Assured of independence, peace and ease.
The honor'd Landlord thus his rights maintains,
And like a Father o'er his Children reigns;
His reign is arbitrary 'tis confess'd,
Because he gains possession of the breast;
And wins the affections, of the gen'rous hind,
By noble dealings and by actions kind;
Who tho' he spurns the mean desire of pelf,
Enriching others meets reward himself.
Of him ye Landlords learn the only way,
To make your Acres your high hopes repay;
And know that only by a lasting lease,
Your lands ye can improve, your wealth increase;
See this plain truth, clear as the solar ray,
In COKE'S large rental, swelling ev'ry day;
Turn but your eyes to HOLKHAM'S fertile plain,
And see it proved in ev'ry joyous swain;
Behold how riches, in a Patriot's hand,
Diffuse abundance thro' a steril land;
And view how wealth, when properly applied,

Scatters her golden lustre far and wide.
Within the narrow space of fifty years;
How Nature's rugged face improv'd appears;
Where scarce a sheep cot rais'd its shelt'ring head,
To screen the Shepherd as his flocks he fed;
Now graceful mansions glad the Traveller's eyes,
And socialize the hills on which they rise;
Where here and there a dome of antique taste,
Made solitude appear amid the waste;
Now ornamental buildings grace the spot,
And population cheers the humble cot:
Where not a briar would rise to deck the heath,
Nor wild *flower* bloom to paint a May day wreath;
Now cooling groves and flowery sweets are seen,
To form a landscape mid' the varied scene;
Within whose sylvan shades we see reside,
In ease, content, and independent pride;
The NORFOLK YEOMEN rearing Heroes brave,
To guard BRITANNIA while she rules the wave;
Just such a *Peasantry* in heart and nerve,
As *England's Genius* glories to preserve.

Amid the fruitful hills and smiling vales,
Each grateful Tenant, his loved Landlord hails;
Whose spacious mansion tow'ring to the skies,
Central we see majestically rise;
Around whose bright demesnes, a happy race
Of wealthy Farmers share the fertile space;
And while they feel his favours grateful glow,
Though from his streams their smaller streamlets flow;
In chrystal currents, gliding pure and clear,
Through all the country round the swains to cheer.
Though his bright beams, just like the orb of day,
The lesser stars eclipses with his ray;
It warms, illumes, and gladdens as it shines,
Each minor Planet which around him twines
While as they circle near their central sun,

Illumin'd by his light their course they run;
Fed from his flame they own his golden rays,
And glisten round him in a silver blaze.

When Heavens indulgence joineth earth to skies,
In nice gradations does the chain arise;
From beast to man, from man the links extend,
Angels to Seraphs rise, and these ascend,
In shining orders, unto us unknown,
All stretching forward to the Empyrean throne;
Yet never destined, in their loftiest flight,
To reach the glorious source of life and light.
Thus if mens acts with Heavens we may compare,
NORFOLK'S GREAT COMMONER his fame would rear;
Lifting the poor Plebeian from the dust,
The chain extending to a place of trust;
The trusty Servant to a Bailiff springs;
The Bailiff sinks, a cheerful Farmer sings;
The Farmer grows in wealth, wealth has no worth,
Until dispers'd among the sons of earth;
His Children rise with wealth, they learning gain,
And knowledge still extends the golden chain;
Wisdom in Virtue ends, and thus he tries
To raise a lowly Peasant to the skies;
Thus imitating Heaven while here below,
Endeavouring so his image fair to show,
In pristine beauty, bursting from the clay,
As from his makers hand, he sprung to day.

* * * * *

Could such a man then in the *shades* remain,
To cheer the heart and bless the labouring swain?
No, worth like his, which Greece or Rome might praise!
Wisdom denied this solace of his days;
And call'd him forth, to glad the noble band,
Of faithful champions for their native land;
To BRITAINS SENATE *Virtue* called her son,
And LIBERTY reviving hail'd her own.

Just at the crisis of that wasteful war,
Which misled Albion proclaim'd afar,
Across the Atlantic wave, where Slaughter stood,
And dyed the British hand with British blood;
Then as the County's Genius look'd around,
To where her worthiest offspring might be found;
Soon HOLKHAM'S glitt'ring turrets she discerned,
Where in her COKE the heart of CATO burned;
There like the good *Cincennatus* at plough,
In olden times, she 'spied her Patriot now;
And call'd him thence, to help the ship of state,
Where frightful rocks, were frowning big with fate;
To guide her safely o'er the threat'ning shoal,
And keep her freightage safe, her timbers whole.
Then love of Country fired his youthful breast;
He flew to save her tho' by foes oppress'd;
The COUNTY roused sustained his cheering voice,
And FIFTY SUMMERS have approv'd her choice.
Placed in the Senate there he joined the few;
Still faithful found among a faithless crew;
Their strength augmenting by his Patriot name,
Which flew before, the Herald of his fame;
Their numbers few in intellect were strong,
For PITT and BURKE were in the minor throng;
There had they kept, had Virtue ruled their hearts,
But pride prevailing tinged their shining parts.

* * * * *

Alas! how few are proof against the wiles,
Of artful Courtiers, fascinating smiles;
Allured by place ambitiously they rise,
And spurn the People and their rights despise;
With hearts ungrateful treating them as foes,
Though the first patrons on whose wings they rose;
But COKE, too good the Virtues to disgrace,
By bartering honour for the sake of place,
Firm to his trust and to the Country true,

The path of justice anxious to pursue;
With ERSKINE, FOX, and ROMILLY the great,
His glory placing in his Country's fate;
Resolved the leaky Vessel, still to trim;
Or, with the stately Bark, to sink or swim.
What though they could not her distress prevent,
They ne'er to cause it have their suffrage lent;
And when they saw the ruin we deplore,
Still strove to save and VIRTUE could no more;
But though they could not stem corruption's tide,
They ne'er upon its golden waves would ride;
And as they fail'd to purify its source,
Still used their efforts to obstruct its course:
Could place or pension, COKE'S support obtain,
He had not sought these tempting lures in vain;
Could titled honours lure his soul astray,
To join Corruption, and his trust betray;
These borrowed glories would on him have shone,
Though not with half the brilliance of his own;
Still all unsullied he preserved his soul,
No bribe could tempt him, nor no power control;
But, like the sailor, faithful to the last,
He nail'd his colours to his country's mast.

* * * * *

When war, taxation, and distress unite
To rouse the COUNTRY and her ire excite;
And a wrong'd People, while their burthens press
Call'd on the Crown for succour and redress;
The minions who prevailed the sword to draw,
For their own safety would *suspend* the law; [16]
And those who dared the People's voice to slight,
Resolved to rob them of their dearest right;
Then did our Patriot pure, resist the act,
With wisdom's *worthiest weapon* REASON back'd;
But all in vain our liberties we mourn,
On false pretences from the Country torn;

Yet still he hoped to see the rising day,
When England's glory, bursting with its ray;
Should shine again, with pristine splendour graced,
Each blot destroyed, and every stain effaced:
Her Sun still burning with fresh glory bright,
And, with her Heavenly beams of warmth and light,
Illume the world, and teach mankind to know;
That VIRTUE, WISDOM, ARTS and SCIENCE grow,
Only where FREEDOM reigns, around whose throne,
These Intellectual gems have ever shone;
For LIBERTY it is, whose beams divine,
Inspire the Sages thought, the Poet's line,
Excite bright genius, spread its golden flame,
And fill a realm with glory, wealth, and fame.

* * * * *

So could Corruption's phalanx rest composed,
While this GREAT COMMONER their acts opposed;
And not attempt to lure him to their side,
By every means which patronage supplied;
The tempting PLACE, the luring TITLE shone,
To make the Patriot his friends disown;
But when they found their efforts all in vain,
The good man to ensnare, his honour stain;
Their Pride was roused, they swell'd with angry heat,
And lent their aid to push him from his seat;
But here again defeated and despised,
They only saw how greatly he was prized;
Who like a mighty rock in ocean cast,
Smiled at the whirlwind, and defied the blast.

* * * * *

Let others boast, the titles *Kings* create;
The flaming riband, or proud coronet;
Honors which wear their glories for a day,
Oft blushing wear, and swiftly fade away:
COKE'S glory found a more substantial base,

Which future Patriots shall delight to trace;
And while the faithful Portrait they pourtray,
See Norfolk's Patriot live in every trait.

* * * * *

For fifty years spent in politic life,
When war and rapine gender'd heat and strife;
No venal act of his appears to wound,
His virtuous soul, or hurt his conscience sound;
No VOTE of his through all that long career,
Has caused the widows sigh, the orphans tear;
Nor from the Peasant's industry withdrawn
Those heavy taxes grievous to be borne;
Curtail'd his Country's rights, the laws denied,
Unto the injured, by oppression tried;
Indemnified the man who did him wrong,
Or made the Oligarchal Tyrants strong;
Nor when the times perplexed a starving poor,
Who sue for pity and for aid implore;
Their sad petitions in such deep distress,
Denied the means of urging for redress;
To their bewailings gave the name of riot,
And crushed their rights, to keep the injured quiet.
Then if the Virtues which adorn his name,
Did not quite fill the trumpet of his fame;
'Twould make no faint addition to the sound,
To tell the acts where he could not be found,
To lend his name, his voice, his vote to raise,
And cloud the Sun of England's better days;
And that which courtiers boastfully have done,
Should be his glory to have left undone.

* * * *

Born for the good of all, his bosom glows,
With softest sympathy in all its' throws;
No narrow feeling e'er restrains his grace,
Whose heart expansive takes in all his race;

No sect or party, rank or state we find,
Contract the bounty of his gen'rous mind;
To human wretchedness his list'ning ear,
Is ever open, and his heart sincere
In gen'rous bounty, wafts the swift relief,
To whom stern mis'ry overloads with grief;
And if he can't restore the broken heart,
His sympathizing bosom bears a part:
Thus sensibility his heart to bless,
In sweet o'erflowings shews its fine impress;
And he who can this balmy balsam share,
The better graces nurtures plump and fair:
It is the soil in which the Virtues grow,
To gild the fields, and paint the vales below;
Sow but the seeds, the germs will quickly shoot,
And grow luxuriant from the fruitful root;
Mature through life, and when the Angels reap,
The ripened harvest, in bright worlds will keep;
For sympathizing feelings warm the breast,
Of heavenly spirits and delight the blest;
And when sweet sympathies the bosom move,
We most resemble Heaven, for Heaven is love.

* * * * *

But cease fond Muse nor longer strive to paint,
His bright perfections with thy pencil faint;
Nor more attempt that conduct to relate,
Which guides the Patriot in a sinking state;
When ev'ry action of his life is lent,
To guard his COUNTRY, or to serve her meant;
Could we retrace the fifty years gone by—
But who can look at them without a sigh;
What act designed our freedom to defend,
Did not his influence and his vote befriend;
What meant to ease the burdens of the land,
Did not his instant patronage command;
The PRESS' LIBERTY, the JURY'S right,

Supporting still, with reasons clearest light,
Sweet PEACE, to keep or to restore her reign,
He deemed no effort lost, no labour vain;
For well he knew protected by her smile,
ARTS, COMMERCE, SCIENCE, *flourish* in our Isle.
When looking back a century or more,
With anxious heart our errors to explore;
The faults he sees desirous to amend,
The People's glory and his Country's friend;
Sought every means which wisdom can suggest,
To keep the fre'est system still the best;
By rectifying ev'ry known abuse,
Which gliding time is apt to introduce,
In the best schemes devised by human skill,
And thus preserve its pristine vigour still,
Has ever been his object, hope and aim,
And from this PUBLIC VIRTUE springs his fame:
And yet no visionary schemer he,
Would ne'er advance beyond what he could see
His wish to mend, but fearful of mistake,
He never wish'd to change for changing sake;
But what experience shows the times require,
Limit his wish and bound his whole desire;
E'en these to gain by gentle means he tries,
By mild expedients, and by measures wise;
Not anxious grasping to get all he sees,
At one rude effort, but by slow degrees;
Nor would he e'er despise what power would grant,
Because he knows it is not all we want;
But takes with joy the good he can obtain,
And hopes in time the residue to gain;
This hope at length the grateful Patriot saw,
Half gratified—by JUSTICE, TRUTH, and LAW;
And though he trembled at the threatened storm,
The tempest saw repelled by MILD REFORM;
And what for fifty years he sought in vain,
Lives to behold in a FOURTH WILLIAM'S reign;

And a NEW CHARTER, destined to endure,
Renders our Rights and Liberties secure:
Then, all his work complete, his duty o'er,
He quits his public toils, resolved no more,
To represent the County, or her weal;
But trust her safety to more youthful zeal;
And with a conduct every where admired,
Resigned his seat and cheerfully retired;
Grateful to find that *friends* and *foes* now own,
That HE to ENGLAND has HIS DUTY DONE.
Still like the glorious orb which gilds the day,
He warms, delights, and blesses with his ray;
Yet silent spreads his bounty as he goes,
Observed but by the favors he bestows.

* * * * *

Hail! to the man who greatly spends his days,
In deeds of glory 'bove the Muse's praise;
With grateful raptures may his heart still glow,
And healthy roses in his face still blow;
Yet may he long survive, ALL Norfolk's pride,
And 'MID THE PEERAGE o'er her weal preside;
This is his due, and should *be* his reward,
Although he does not much the boon regard;
'Tis only just his Patriot brows should wear,
The dazzling coronet which decks a Peer;
For though the bauble he may wisely slight,
It sometimes dignifies, and wears so bright:
The man it *graces*, and exalts so high,
Among the glitt'ring stars which gild the sky;
That those who wear it as it was designed,
Are raised to Gods among the humbler kind:
Still some will think who most his merits scan,
He'd better live and die the PEOPLES' MAN;
And still be called, acknowledged, and believed,
The greatest Commoner who ever lived;
And that which won the plaudits of the wise,

Through life; remain his glory when he dies.
O may his vigorous frame feel no decay,
But heat receding gently wear away;
His hopes still *bright'ning* as he views the tomb,
While *Virtue's* beams, his closing scene illume;
And, like the day star in the rubied west,
Shine FULLER, LOVELIER, as he sinks to rest.
When rising 'mong the spheres his spirit soars,
As highest Heaven's Empyrean he explores;
Glides 'mid the stars, surveys the milky way,
Exulting in the bright celestial day;
Then may *indulgent* Heaven delight his shade,
With aided ken, the curtain to pervade,
Which hides the realms ethereal from our sight,
And that bright region clouds with shades of night;
So from his glory in yon azure sky,
He still his earthly Paradise shall 'spy;
There see his Heirs adorn the name of COKE,
And all the COUNTY *still to* HOLKHAM *look*:
Behold a race of Patriots from him rise,
In training there, to meet him in the skies:
Still join unseen among her festive guests;
And feel the rapture which delights their breasts:
Enjoy THIS PARADISE, or *Heaven* at *will*,
The GUARDIAN GENIUS of his HOLKHAM STILL.

FINIS.

FOOTNOTES

[16] The Suspension of the HABEAS CORPUS ACT.
